CONTENTS

What is a screw?	4
Spirals	6
Lids and tops	8
Nuts and bolts	10
Screwdrivers and corkscrews	12
Screws are strong	14
Changing a wheel	16
Water tap	18
Drills and borers	20
Boring a tunnel	22
Water screws	24
Aircraft propellers	26
Make a wind propeller	28
Glossary	30
Answers to questions	31
Index	32

What is a screw?

Some screws are long and others are short. But they all have a spiral thread.

Screws are used to join one thing to another. Look around you. You may not notice many screws straightaway, but look closer. The legs of chairs, tables and cupboards are often screwed on. Door **hinges** are screwed into the door frame. Different parts of television sets, computers and cars are screwed together, too.

Did you know?

Screws were first used instead of nails about 500 years ago. But the first known screw was invented just over 2200 years ago by a Greek mathematician called Archimedes. He invented a huge screw that lifted water from one level to another.

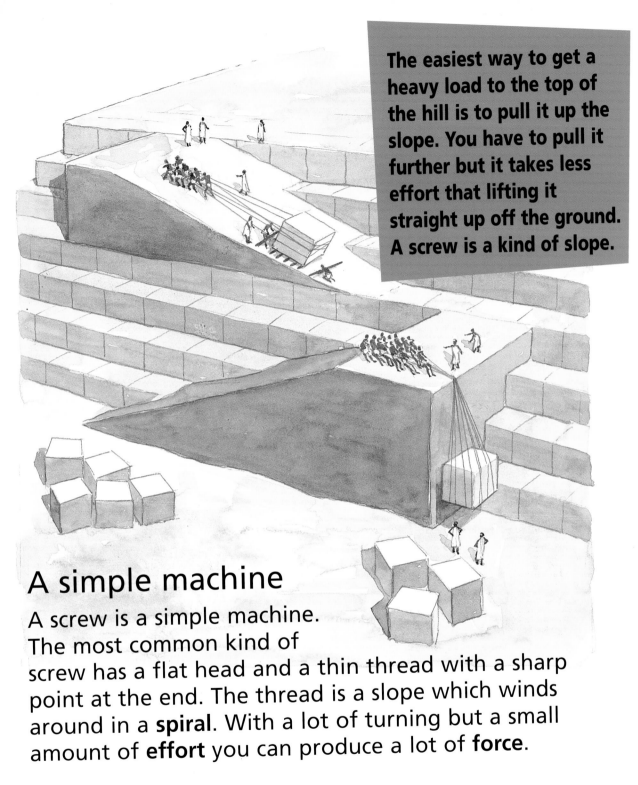

The easiest way to get a heavy load to the top of the hill is to pull it up the slope. You have to pull it further but it takes less effort that lifting it straight up off the ground. A screw is a kind of slope.

A simple machine

A screw is a simple machine. The most common kind of screw has a flat head and a thin thread with a sharp point at the end. The thread is a slope which winds around in a **spiral**. With a lot of turning but a small amount of **effort** you can produce a lot of **force**.

A screw is so simple, you may not think of it as a machine. Levers, wheels, springs, ramps and pulleys are also simple machines. This book will show you how useful screws are. It looks at how different kinds of screws work and how we use them.

Spirals

A **spiral** is a slope which moves up and around in a circle. A screw works because it has a spiral thread, but other things use spirals too. Multi-storey carparks often have a curved slope for cars to drive from one floor to another. The curve makes a long, gentle slope that is easy to drive up and down. A helter-skelter is a spiral slope that you slide down.

This water slide is in the shape of a spiral. You slide round and round the slope and splash into the pool at the bottom. You slide around a long way to drop a short distance.

It takes less effort to climb the steps of a spiral staircase than it would to climb a ladder. The spiral spreads the climbing over a longer distance.

Spiral staircase

A spiral staircase has more steps than a ladder of the same height. The shallower the step the easier it is to climb. In a spiral staircase, you walk a long way around to climb a short way up.

A spiral staircase takes up much less space than a long, straight flight of stairs so it is usually used where there is not much space. Round towers and lighthouses, for example, have spiral staircases.

Try this!

Turn a straight slope into a spiral. Cut a square of paper in half along the diagonal, to give you a triangle. Place a pencil along one of the shorter sides of the triangle. Roll the paper around the pencil towards the opposite corner. The long side of the triangle makes a spiral around the pencil.

Lids and tops

A screw cap or lid makes a tight **seal**. The **spiral** screw on the bottle fits into the spiral groove inside the top. The screw pulls the lid down onto the seal. It fits so tightly that no liquid can leak out.

A bottle of fizzy drink has a screw cap to stop the gas inside escaping. When you have poured a drink you must screw the cap back on to stop the drink going flat. You turn the cap a long way around to push the lid down a short way.

The spiral thread inside the cap of the bottle exactly fits over the spiral thread at the top of the bottle.

Make it work!

Some bottles have a cork instead of a cap. The cork is slightly wider than the top of the bottle. When it is pushed into the bottle it is squashed tightly against the glass. Try to push a cork back into a bottle. Which is easier – pushing in the cork or screwing on a cap?

Each of these jars has a screw-on lid. The screw makes a tight fit which helps to keep the food inside fresh.

Jars

Many jars have screw lids. The lid makes an airtight seal to keep the food inside clean and fresh. If jam is not sealed it dries out and may go **mouldy**. If coffee is not sealed, it loses some of its taste. What do you think might happen to the gherkins if the lid is loose?

9

Nuts and bolts

Nuts and bolts are used to hold things together. They join the wheels to a bicycle and they sometimes hold the different bars of a climbing frame together. Nuts and bolts are so strong that they are used to hold the engine in place inside a car.

A nut and bolt joins the wheel to the bicycle frame. A spanner is used to tighten the nut.

A nut and the bolt both have a **spiral** thread, like a screw bottle top. The bolt is pushed through the two holes in the bars of the frame, and the nut is screwed on tightly.

10

Think about it!

The size of a nut must match the size of the bolt. Which bolt would fit the large nut on the bottom right? Which bolt would fit the wing nut above it?

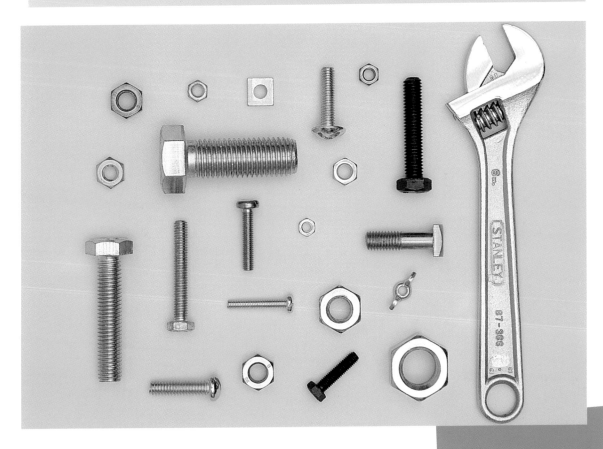

Spanner

Some nuts have wings on each side to help you turn them, but most nuts are tightened with a **spanner**. The spanner is a **lever** that fits over the nut. The longer the spanner the easier it is to turn the nut. Some spanners can be adjusted to fit the size of any nut. Look at the spanner in this photo. Can you see what is used to adjust the size?

The outside of the nut can be any shape, but most are hexagonal. Why do you think that is so?

11

Screwdrivers and corkscrews

You cannot push a screw into hard wood using just your fingers. You have to use a **screwdriver** instead. The tip of the screwdriver fits into a slot or a small cross carved into the top. As you turn the screwdriver, it grips the screw and makes it turn, too. As the screw turns, the sharp thread cuts a spiral groove in the wood. The thread grips the groove tightly.

Each time the screwdriver turns the screw all the way around, the screw moves a short way into the wood.

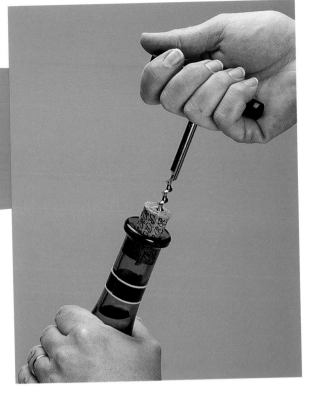

A cork fits tightly inside the neck of the bottle. To get the cork out, you have to twist the corkscrew into the cork and then pull hard!

Magnifying effort

A screwdriver magnifies your **effort**. The effort you put into turning the handle is concentrated on the tip of the screwdriver. And the **force** applied to the head of the screw is turned into an even bigger force at the point of the screw.

A corkscrew works like a screw and screwdriver combined. As you turn the handle of the corkscrew, the screw bites a deep groove into the cork. The screw grips the cork all along the groove. When you pull the handle up, the cork slips out with a pop of air!

Make it work!

Use a spare piece of soft wood, some screws and a screwdriver. Try to push the screw into the wood with your fingers. Now use the screwdriver. How far into the wood can you drive the screw? Be careful – the end of the screwdriver is sharp.

Screws are strong

Each screw is only 3 centimetres long but together they can hold up these shelves of books.

Screws are incredibly strong. Several small screws can hold up a shelf of books. The screws are short but each one grips the wall so tightly, the heavy weight of books will not pull them out. A few screws can take the weight of a heavy door, thick curtains, a large mirror or a cupboard. Look to see what is hanging by a few screws in your home.

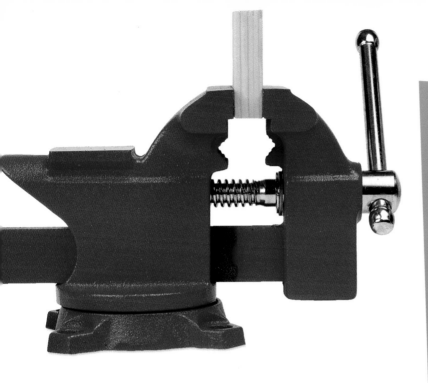

Vices and clamps are used in workshops to grip pieces of wood and other things. The handle turns the screw until the jaws of the vice or clamp press tightly against the wood.

Vices and clamps

A **vice** uses a screw to hold things firmly. For example, it holds wood completely steady while it is being sawed. It holds a piece of metal steady while it is bent or hammered. The vice has two jaws. Turning the handle turns the screw to move one jaw towards the other.

A clamp works in the same way as a vice. Shoe-menders use clamps when they glue a new sole to a shoe. The clamp squeezes the two parts together while the glue dries.

Think about it!

Why do you think most screws are made of metal? What would happen if a screw was made of wax or plaster?

Changing a wheel

All cars carry a spare wheel and a bag of tools in case one of the tyres gets a puncture. When that happens the tools are used to change the wheel. First the car has to be lifted using a car **jack**.

A small jack can lift one side of a car. As the handle turns the screw, the arm of the jack lifts up, taking the car with it.

The jack fits into a special plate under the car and a handle is attached to the end of the screw. You have to turn the handle many times to lift the car just a little. In fact, the handle moves about 50 times further than the car!

16

Wheel nuts

Once the tyre is off the ground, the wheel can be removed. Each wheel is held on by four or five nuts and bolts. The nuts are so tight, it can take a lot of **effort** to loosen them, even with the car's special **spanner**. When the old wheel is off, the spare wheel is screwed on tight. The jack is wound down and the car is ready to go.

Make it work!

Design a machine that you could use to lift a friend or even an adult. It does not have to lift very high. What else could your machine be used for?

Water tap

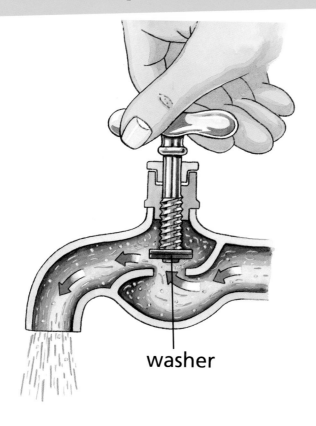

washer

When you turn the tap on, water from the pipe flows under the washer and out of the tap.

How many times a day do you turn on a tap to get some water? When you have a bath, you turn the taps full on and the water pours out. To wash your hands or get a drink of water, you turn the tap a little to let the water flow more slowly.

Try this!

Feel for yourself how powerful a tap and washer are. Turn on a tap or garden hose and put your thumb over the spout. Can you stop the water flowing? The screw in the tap can!

How a tap works

The handle of the tap is joined to a large screw with a round, rubber disc on the end. The disc is called a **washer**. Turning the handle turns the screw and moves the washer up and down. The washer is like a plug which fits over a hole inside the tap.

When the washer is up, water flows through the hole and out of the tap. As you turn the tap off, the washer begins to block the hole, and the water flows more slowly. The water only stops flowing, when the washer blocks the hole completely.

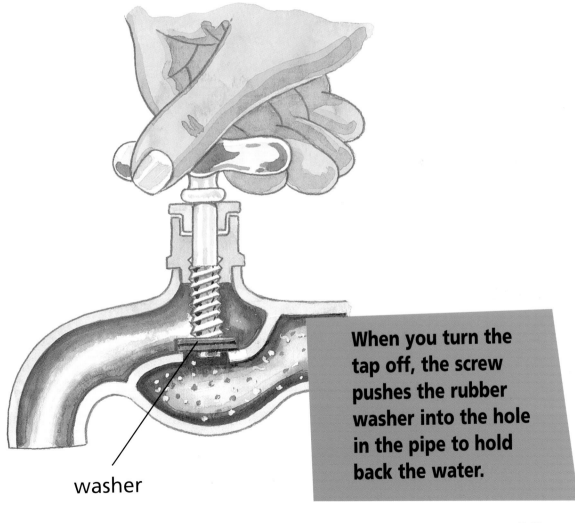

washer

When you turn the tap off, the screw pushes the rubber washer into the hole in the pipe to hold back the water.

Drills and borers

As the drill bit spins round, the sharp point bites into the wood. The wider the drill bit, the wider the hole.

Drills are used to bore holes in wood, metal, plastic and even the ground. A drill has a sharp point and a spiral screw. As the drill turns, the point breaks up the material to bore the hole. The loose material is pushed along the **spiral** out of the hole.

An electric drill spins fast and works quickly. Most people use an electric drill when they want to screw something into the wall. If you tried to fix a screw straight into a **plasterboard** wall, the plaster would crumble. Instead the drill makes a hole which is filled with a plastic plug. The screw is then driven into the plug.

20

This huge drill is called a pile driver. It is drilling a deep hole to make concrete foundations for a building.

Borers

Huge machines called borers and pile drivers dig deep holes through the ground. The huge screw on the end is called an **auger**. As the engine turns the auger, it breaks up the earth and the spiral screw fills with mud. The auger is then lifted up to the surface. It spins again and the mud flies off.

Did you know?

Huge drills bore through soil and thick layers of rock to reach oil trapped deep below the ground. These drills may burrow 7000 metres (25,000 feet) through the rocks. This is nearly as deep as the height of the world's highest mountains.

Boring a tunnel

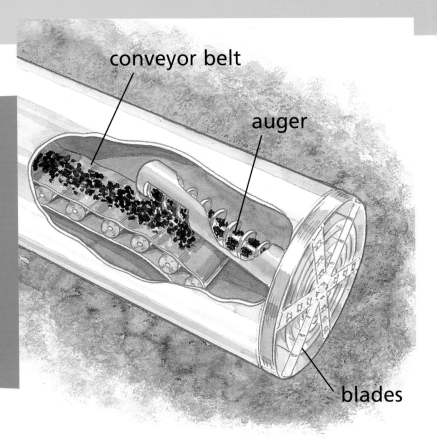

conveyor belt

auger

blades

A mechanical mole tunnels through soil and soft rock. The loose material passes onto a spinning auger which carries it up to a conveyor belt.

Most cities have tunnels deep below the ground that carry away waste water from buildings and the streets. Even bigger tunnels have been bored to carry roads and railways through mountains, such as the Alps in Switzerland and the Rocky Mountains in North America.

Tunnel borers are huge machines that cut through soil and rocks to dig tunnels. Sharp blades at the front of a tunnel borer spin around and cut through the rock like a giant drill. As the machine inches forward, the loose rock and earth is passed back through the blades and onto a **conveyor belt**.

The Channel Tunnel

The Channel Tunnel was bored through rock under the sea between France and Britain. You can now travel by train from London to Paris. Huge machines bored the two main railway tunnels. Each was longer than two football pitches and moved forwards about one metre (one yard) every hour.

This kind of machine helped to bore the Channel Tunnel under the sea. Huge blades at the front of the machine cut through the rock. The broken rock passes through the blades straight onto a conveyor belt, which loads it onto a train.

Did you know?

The world's longest transport tunnel is the Seikan rail tunnel. It is 53.8 kilometres (33.4 miles) long and travels under the sea to link the Japanese islands of Honshu and Hokkaido.

Water screws

This water pump is called an Archimedes screw because it was invented by Archimedes over 2000 years ago. The farmer turns the handle to raise water from the river onto his field.

An Archimedes screw is a kind of **pump**. Inside is an **auger**. As the handle is turned the water is wound up the pump. It spurts out of the top and into a ditch or trough.

Think about it!

It might seem strange that a ship moves forward by pushing water backwards, but you do the same thing when you swim. How do you push the water backwards to move yourself forwards through the water?

Propellers

A **propeller** is a kind of screw. The blades are curved and slanted. As they turn they **spiral** through the water and push the boat forward. The propellers are tiny compared with the size of the ship, but the action of these screws is so powerful, two propellers can drive a huge ship.

As the propellers on the back of the ship spin round the blades push the water backwards. This in turn pushes the ship forward.

The propeller turns clockwise to push the boat forward. The boat can be made to move backwards by turning the propeller the other way. Since a boat does not have brakes, the quickest way to stop it going forward is to turn the propellers into reverse.

Aircraft propellers

The **propeller** on an aircraft works like that on a ship. The blades are twisted so that, as they spin round, they pull the aeroplane through the air. They are driven round by the engine and screw through the air like a metal screw pushing into wood.

A propeller pulls this plane through the air. The propeller is turned by an engine.

Try this!

Cut a piece of paper like this: and then fold it like this: Put a paperclip on the end. Now stand on a chair and drop the paper. What happens?

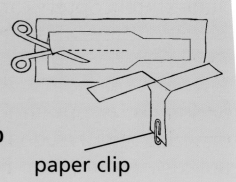

paper clip

The blades of the helicopter act like a propeller to move it through the air.

Helicopter

A helicopter has three or more large blades. The blades are wings as well as propellers. As they spin they keep the helicopter up and push it through the air.

Unlike an aeroplane, a helicopter can move backwards and sideways as well as forwards. The pilot changes direction by changing the tilt of the blades. Helicopters can move straight up and down so they can take off and land on a very small space.

A helicopter can also hover in one spot. They are often used to rescue people from ships or cliff faces. An ambulance helicopter can airlift people straight to a landing site on a hospital roof.

Make a wind propeller

This toy uses a **propeller** to spin in the wind or when you blow on it. The propeller is a screw and it will work best if you use a metal screw to fix it to the stick.

You will need:

- Stiff paper or thin card
- Ruler
- Masking tape
- A stick at least a centimetre thick
- A small thin screw
- Pencil, scissors

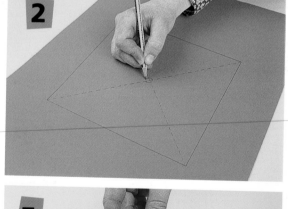

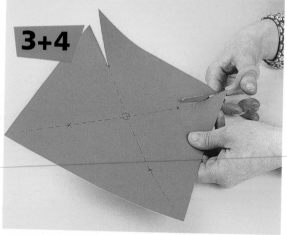

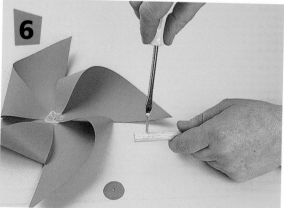

1   Draw a square 20 centimetres by 20 centimetres onto the paper or card.

2   Join the opposite corners with a dotted line. Draw a small circle around the point where the two diagonals cross.

3   Use a ruler to measure the halfway point between the centre and each corner. Make a small cross for each.

4   Cut out the square and cut down each diagonal as far as the small cross.

5   Fold each corner in turn over so that it touches the outside of the centre circle. Tape each corner down to make a propeller.

6   Place the propeller at the top of the stick. Push the screw through the centre and into the wood to hold the propeller firmly in place. Make sure the propeller can spin freely.

7   Hold the toy in front of you and blow on the propeller. It should spin round.

Glossary

airtight made so that air cannot get in or out

auger large tool for boring holes

conveyor belt a wide, flat loop that turns around to carry something from one end to the other

drill a tool for boring holes

drill bit the spiral screw on the end of the drill

effort the force applied to make something move

force a push, pull or twist that makes something move

hexagonal having six sides of equal length

hinge two metal plates joined together so that they can turn to open and close

jack a tool for lifting a heavy weight, such as a car

lever a simple machine which is usually used to lift or balance something

magnifies makes larger

mouldy covered with a fungus and beginning to rot

plasterboard a board made of plaster and felt used to make walls inside a building

propeller curved blades which turn around to push a plane through the air or a boat through the water

pump a machine for lifting water

screwdriver a tool for driving a screw into wood or other material

seal something that fits so tightly neither gas nor liquid can get in or out

spanner a tool for turning a nut on a bolt in order to loosen or tighten the nut

spiral a slope that circles up or down

vice a tool that uses a screw to hold something very tightly

washer a flat ring that makes a tight seal in a tap

Answers to questions

p9 If the lid of the gherkins is loose, the liquid might dry out and the gherkins go bad. And, if the jar was knocked over, the liquid would spill out.

p11 The adjustable **spanner** uses a spiral thread, like a screw to adjust the end to the size of the nut.

p11 The outside of a nut is usually **hexagonal** because it is easier to grip it with the spanner. If it was round it would slip.

p11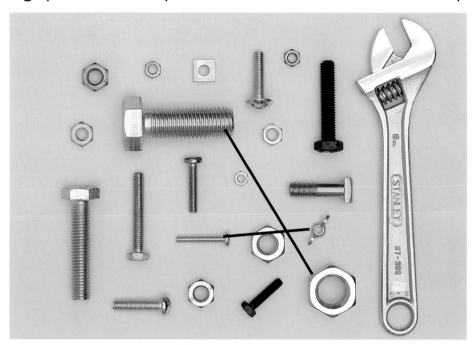

The big bolt would fit the nut on the lower right. The longer thin bolt would fit the wing nut.

p15 Screws are made of metal because it is strong. Wax and plaster would crumble.

p24 When you swim you pull the water backwards with your arms and push it backwards as you kick or move your feet and legs.

p26 The propeller spins as it drops. Notice that it always spins anticlockwise.

Index

aeroplane 26
aircraft 26–27
Archimedes 4, 24
auger 21, 24, 30

bolt 10–11, 17
borers 21, 22–23
bicycle 10

car 10, 16–17
changing a car wheel
    16–17
Channel Tunnel 23
clamp 15
cork 9, 13
corkscrew 13

drill 20–21, 30

electric drill 20

foundations 21

helicopter 27
helter-skelter 6

jack 16, 30
jar 9

mechanical mole 23
metal screws 4, 5, 12, 15
multi-storey carpark 6

nut 10–11, 17

oil 21

pile driver 21
propeller 25, 26–27,
    28–29, 30
pump 24, 30

screw top 8–9
screwdriver 12–13, 30
Seikan rail tunnel 23
shelf 14
ship 24, 25
simple machine 5
shoe-mender 15
slope 5
spanner 10–11, 17, 30
spiral staircase 7
spirals 6–7, 30

tap 18–19
tunnel borer 22–23
tunnels 22–23

vice 15, 30

washer 18, 19, 30
water 6, 18–19, 24, 25
water slide 6
wheel nut 17
wing nut 11